NOT
A
CONQUERED
PEOPLE:

Two Carolinians View Parliamentary Taxation

THE McNEIL CENTER FOR
EARLY AMERICAN
S T U D I E S

For

Don Higginbotham

NOT
A
CONQUERED
PEOPLE:

Two Carolinians View Parliamentary Taxation

by

William S. Price, Jr.

Raleigh 1975

George Grenville, Architect of the Stamp Act

Photo: Archives and History

TABLE OF CONTENTS

John Collet, Map of North Carolina, 1770
Photo: Archives and History

INTRODUCTORY ESSAY

When the British Parliament passed the Stamp Act in March, 1765, to become effective in November, few Englishmen realized that they were lighting the fuse of a powder keg. The legislation placed a small tax on certain items such as newspapers, pamphlets, insurance policies, licenses, ship's papers, playing cards, dice, and, perhaps most importantly, legal documents. Never before had Parliament imposed such a direct tax on the colonies. Revenues collected were designed to pay a portion of the cost of maintaining British troops in the American colonies for defensive purposes. However, numerous colonists disliked the notion of a standing army in their country. More significantly, they feared that this small tax might be the first of many; for once the principle of "taxation without representation" was established, an irreversible precedent would be fixed.

During the summer of 1765 there were violent demonstrations in opposition to the Stamp Act in most of the American colonies. Leading colonial thinkers engaged in a paper war over the act as pamphlets, on both sides of the taxation issue, poured from the presses. Pamphlets were especially suited to this kind of ideological controversy. Inexpensive to buy and flexible in size, they appealed to the reading public of the 1760s. Writers could develop their ideas more fully in pamphlets of ten to fifty pages than in the limited space of a newspaper article.[1]

In October, 1765, delegates from nine of the thirteen provinces met in New York City for the Stamp Act Congress and urged repeal of the hated measure. (Governor William Tryon successfully blocked the election of delegates from North Carolina to that meeting.) The representatives resolved to oppose any tax not levied by their own legislatures, and their firm conviction resounded across the Atlantic. In addition, Americans retaliated by refusing to import most European goods, thereby causing a decline in British exports; and a number of English merchants joined the colonists in their fight for repeal

1

of the act. Faced with such opposition, Parliament decided to revoke the Stamp Act in March, 1766.[2]

The two pamphlets offered here demonstrate the extremes to which opinions of parliamentary taxation differed in the American colonies. Although the authors of these two works did not know one another at the time each wrote his pamphlet, they soon became associated through mutual service on the North Carolina Superior Court — Martin Howard as chief justice and Maurice Moore as an associate justice. Howard was not a resident of North Carolina at the time he wrote *A Letter from a Gentleman at Halifax to His Friend in Rhode Island,* but less than two years after its publication he was one of the colony's leading officials. In their contradictory views of parliamentary taxation, Howard and Moore illuminate the mental turmoil confronting many Americans in 1765. Should the colonies submit to what was, after all, a tiny tax; or should they insist that they not be taxed without their consent? Out of this dilemma grew much of the intellectual basis for resistance to England and, ultimately, for the Revolution itself. Likewise, the Stamp Act crisis of 1765-1766 showed the colonists that they could unite in a common purpose in a way they had been unable to do in their previous wars with the French.[3] In a political and intellectual sense, the Stamp Act crisis was a major progenitor of the American Revolution.

In order to understand *how* Howard and Moore were moved to write their respective pamphlets, it is helpful to examine their careers individually in some detail. Then in the hope of explaining *why* they wrote as they did, it is necessary to compare the similarities and differences of the two men — first, Howard.

Martin Howard was born either in England or New England about 1725 but grew up in Rhode Island since his father, Martin, Sr., was admitted as a freeman of Newport in May, 1726.[4] Young Howard read law in Newport under James Honyman, Jr., later attorney general of Rhode Island. One of his biographers wrote that he studied at an English Inn of Court, but Howard is not listed in Jones's *American Members of the Inns of Court.*[5] On December 29, 1749, he married his first wife, Ann Brenton Conklin of South Kingstown, Rhode Island. They had three children — a son and two daughters. Although a regular attendant at Newport's Anglican Trinity Church, Howard was reared an Anabaptist and was not baptized an Anglican until the summer of 1770 in North Carolina.[6]

During 1752-1755 he served as librarian of the famed Redwood Library. The Rhode Island legislature chose him as a delegate to the Albany Congress in June, 1754, to negotiate with the Six Nations of northern Indians in the coming hostilities with France. In 1756 Howard was elected to the Rhode Island Assembly and four years later served on the committee to revise the laws of the colony.[7]

During the turbulent years after the close of the French and Indian War in 1763, Howard was a member of the conservative Newport Club, which included such figures as Peter Harrison, the architect, and Dr. Thomas Moffat, a sometime political essayist. These men abhorred the disorder of Rhode Island politics, and in April, 1764, Howard joined with Moffat in a newspaper campaign to have the colony's charter revoked and royal government imposed. As a part of this effort, Howard corresponded with Benjamin Franklin, who was then trying to accomplish the same end in Pennsylvania. In February, 1765, Howard authored the pamphlet, *A Letter from a Gentleman at Halifax to His Friend in Rhode Island.* In it he responded to a pamphlet by Governor Stephen Hopkins of the previous November which, among other things, had criticized the Newport Club. The thrust of Howard's essay, however, was support of Parliament's authority to tax the colonies. Although Howard had not been named as author on the pamphlet's title page, there was no doubt among his friends or enemies that he had written it.[8] Undoubtedly when he was attacked as a Stamp Act agent in the summer of 1765, much of the hatred vented against Howard stemmed from his identification as the "Gentleman at Halifax."

When leaders of the Stamp Act riots (which occurred in Newport on August 27-28, 1765) formulated their plans, they reserved a special enmity for Howard, whose pamphlet alleged that Newport merchants were little better than smugglers. On the morning of August 27, a gallows was erected near Colony House in Newport with effigies of Rhode Island's three stamp agents hanging there. Crowds gathered and by 5 o'clock in the afternoon free drinks were provided. After sunset the three figures were cut down and burned.[9] That evening Howard was walking through town with John Robinson, the customs officer, when Robinson was assaulted by a small crowd. Howard helped rescue his friend and then upbraided the ruffians for their behavior.[10] The next evening a mob with painted faces and broad axes broke into Howard's house, demolished his furniture, and drank the contents of his wine cellar. Later that night they returned to his home, smashed his doors, floors, and windows and even cut down the trees in his front yard. By August 29 Howard was so concerned for his own safety and that of his family that he boarded the British ship *Cygnet* and two days later sailed for England arriving there in October.[11] Seven years later while in North Carolina, Howard submitted a claim for £524 13s. sterling to the Rhode Island legislature for his losses in the riots. The assembly lowered the award to £111 18s. but never paid it. In a swipe at Howard as a defender of the crown, the legislature agreed to pay his award when England fully recompensed Rhode Island for its role in the French and Indian War.[12] After demonstrating the extent of his losses and protesting his loyalty to friends in England, the crown offered Howard the chief justiceship of North Carolina. He accepted, and his commission was issued on July 29, 1766.[13]

By January, 1767, Howard was in North Carolina and on the twenty-third of the month qualified as chief justice before the governor and council. At some time during the year he went to Boston to marry his second wife, Abigail Greenleaf, daughter of the sheriff of Suffolk County, Massachusetts. While there he sat for his portrait by John Singleton Copley.[14]

Having escaped from a volatile situation in Rhode Island only a short time before, Howard soon found himself in the midst of the regulator upheaval in North Carolina. He presided over all higher-court trials of regulators in the fall of 1768 and generally was considered to have been fair by backcountry residents.[15] In fact when the regulators planned to disrupt the Salisbury court sessions of March, 1771, they specifically excluded the chief justice from their hatred but not his colleagues. In the spring of 1771 he presided at the trials of the rebel leaders of the Battle of Alamance, six of whom were executed.[16]

In January, 1770, Governor Tryon nominated Howard to a seat on the royal council; and on November 19, 1770, he was sworn in.[17] Faithful in his attendance at council sessions, Howard usually sided with the governor especially in the crucial months prior to the Revolutionary War. When the superior court system was suspended in late 1772, Howard served as chief justice of the prerogative courts which Governor Josiah Martin established, but his income from fees was diminished. His salary of £70 per year had not been paid since 1770, although he had averaged at least £800 a year in fees and other perquisites.[18] Lorenzo Sabine writes that in the summer of 1777, Howard said: "I shall have no argument with the Sons of Liberty of Newport; it was they who made me Chief Justice of North Carolina, with a thousand pounds sterling a year."[19] Because of his association with the hated prerogative courts, Howard was the most despised official in the colony (next to the governor) by the summer of 1775. Yet when full-scale fighting broke out, Howard was able to withdraw quietly to his plantation, Richmond, on the Neuse River in Craven County. There he lived a remote existence as his letter thanking James Iredell for a personal kindness in May, 1777, indicates: "An instance of civility to an obscure man in the woods, is as flattering as a compliment to a worn-out beauty. . . . I have lately been so little accustomed even to the common courtesies of life that a sentiment of kindness comes upon me by surprise."[20] By mid-summer it became necessary for Howard to leave North Carolina when he refused to take an oath of loyalty to the state. He moved his family to New York, and less than a year later, went on to England and settled in Middlesex County. Howard was awarded a pension of £250 per year for his loyalty by the British government. In November, 1781, he died and was buried at Chelsea, England.[21]

Maurice Moore was the son of Colonel Maurice and Mary Porter Moore. Born in New Hanover County about 1735, he obtained his early education in New England.[22] His father and his uncle Roger had been among the earliest settlers of the Lower Cape Fear region and were two of the wealthiest men in the colony. By 1757 young Maurice, back in North Carolina, was elected to the lower house of assembly during 1757-1759, 1762, 1764, 1766-1768, 1770-1771, and 1773. In December, 1757, Governor Arthur Dobbs recommended him for membership on the royal council and cited him as an assemblyman who showed "a good disposition to support his Majesty's Interest." During the next six years the governor attempted unsuccessfully to obtain a permanent upper house seat for the young man.[23] On April 24, 1760, Dobbs made an emergency appointment of Moore to the council to insure a quorum. Moore willingly resigned a lower house seat to accept the socially prestigious council chair, and he served there dutifully for a year until a commissioned councillor arrived to displace him.[24] Once back in the assembly, he sought a leading role there, including the speakership; but it always eluded him. Like other members of his family, Moore was an ambitious man.

In January, 1763, the governor and council made Moore an associate justice of the Superior Court.[25] Except for this two-year suspension beginning in 1766, Moore served as judge in superior courts until their collapse late in 1772. Therefore by 1765 Moore was one of the leading young men in the colony.

Like many of his friends and associates in the Lower Cape Fear region, Moore was displeased by passage of the Stamp Act in the summer of 1765. Demonstrations against the act occurred in Wilmington on October 19 and 31. On November 16, Dr. William Houston, who was stamp distributor for North Carolina, was compelled to resign his office by a mob of nearly four hundred people in Wilmington. Among the leaders of this demonstration was James Moore, Maurice's brother, who would later be a general in the Continental Army. Sometime during the summer of 1765, Maurice Moore wrote his pamphlet entitled *The Justice and Policy of Taxing the American Colonies in England* and, unlike Martin Howard, made no attempt to disguise his authorship. Moore's name appeared boldly on the title page.[26] In the pamphlet Moore demonstrated a thorough reading in constitutional law and history as well as tightly

6

reasoned arguments. His essay provided the intellectual framework for resistance in the Lower Cape Fear. When the hated stamps arrived at the mouth of the river on November 28, 1765, there was no one to receive them because of Houston's resignation. Without them no goods could leave port, and the maritime population of Wilmington and Brunswick began to suffer for its principles. Anger peaked early in 1766 when citizens of the Lower Cape Fear learned that their ports were the only ones still closed in America. Elsewhere compliant officials had allowed commerce to resume by issuing certificates that stamps were not available. In February, 1766, there were large protest demonstrations in Wilmington, but potential violence was averted when Parliament repealed the Stamp Act in March.[27] Moore's prominence as an opponent of the Stamp Act led Governor William Tryon to suspend him from his judgeship early in 1766. Tryon characterized the pamphleteer's influence as local: "He is a leading man in this river [Cape Fear] though he enjoys no great share of popularity in other parts of the province."[28]

After repeal of the Stamp Act, tempers in the colony cooled; and in March, 1768, Tryon restored Moore to his judgeship citing his proper conduct since the suspension.[29] The justice thus had returned to the bench during one of the most crucial periods in the life of the colony — the regulator troubles. During Tryon's first expedition into the backcountry in the summer of 1768, Moore served as colonel of a troop of Gentlemen Volunteer Light Dragoons. In September he joined Martin Howard and Richard Henderson at the Salisbury Superior Court where several regulators were tried. Most of these men were acquitted, but at least two leaders were convicted.[30] For a brief time there was an uneasy calm in the backcountry; but on March 13, 1770, Moore reported to the governor that sheriffs in many western counties could neither collect taxes nor serve writs because of regulator agitation.[31]

As unrest continued to grow in the backcountry, Moore chaired a committee of the legislature on December 10, 1770, which called for stern measures to curtail the regulators. Shortly after this action, Samuel Johnston introduced the notorious Riot Act which would serve as one of the legal bases of the Battle of Alamance. On December 20, the General Assembly expelled Herman Husband, the regulator leader, from its membership as publisher (or possibly author) of a libelous letter from James Hunter to Moore printed in the *North Carolina Gazette* on December 14. The letter purported to answer an earlier letter from Moore (which does not now exist) in which he blamed Hunter and Husband for most of the backcountry agitation. Soon after Husband's expulsion, violence flared in several western counties.[32]

Significantly, Moore requested that Tryon allow him to join his associates for the March Superior Court term in Salisbury. By March 18, 1771, the justices reported that it would be unwise to attempt to hold the Hillsborough session of the court because of the volatile situation there. Regulators who had gathered around Salisbury at the time said they were willing for Martin Howard to hold court in the backcountry but not his associates Richard Henderson or Moore. While some of this bias was because Henderson and Moore were commissioned by the despised Tryon and Howard by the king, several regulators expressed a special hatred for Moore and hoped for a chance to flog him.[33] When the three justices were summoned to Hillsborough on May 30, 1771, they sentenced to death twelve regulators taken at the Battle of Alamance (only six were executed); and backcountry resistance ended. By August of the following year, Moore joined with Howard and Henderson in urging an end to prosecution of regulators.[34] If Moore, under the pseudonym Atticus, authored a letter attacking Tryon in the *Virginia Gazette* of November 7, 1771, then he had acquired even earlier a distaste for further punishment of the regulators. F. X. Martin attributed authorship of the Atticus letter to Moore in his 1829 *History of North Carolina from the Earliest Period* and subsequent historians usually have accepted his verdict, but Martin offered no documentation for his statement.[35]

With the general collapse of the colony's court system in 1772, Moore accepted a role as judge in Governor Martin's specially commissioned courts of oyer and terminer. However, Moore contributed to the demise of this temporary scheme when he pointed out technical irregularities in the court's commission at the summer term of 1774 in Wilmington.[36] As revolutionary fervor grew, Moore seemed to be a firm supporter of the patriot cause. He served as a delegate to the provincial congress in Hillsborough on August 20, 1775. While there he was active on several committees and signed the August 23 resolution protesting taxation but affirming loyalty to the king. Although he was elected to the congress at Halifax on November 12, 1776, he did not attend.[37] Two of his sons, Alfred and Maurice, served in the patriot army; and the latter was killed by the British at Brunswick early in 1776. Moore's daughter, Sarah, was the wife of General Francis Nash; and his brother, James, was a patriot general.[38]

Yet there is some evidence that Moore was not wholly committed to the Revolution. On January 9, 1776, he wrote Governor Josiah Martin stating his belief that the people of North Carolina would welcome a return to the *status quo ante* the Stamp Act. He urged the governor to call an assembly to deal with the matter. Martin answered the letter two days later suggesting that he and Moore meet personally to discuss the issue, but they never did.[39] To what extent Moore was vacillating in his support for the Revolution is unclear. In May, 1777, Josiah Martin said that Moore had hoped to propose a plan of reconciliation in January, 1776. He then went on to criticize Moore as "a whimsical visionary in politics . . . strongly tinctured with republicanism." The former governor indicated that Moore longed for a larger role in affairs of state than he was able to achieve. In two decades of service in the lower house of assembly, Moore had never carried a single major point, nor had he gained the speakership he so desired.[40] To add to the confusion, Moore may have written the January 9 letter with the foreknowledge of the Wilmington Committee of Safety.[41] In any case, like many Americans he hesitated to undertake a full scale war with the mother country. In a career replete with some puzzling contradictions (his desire for high office but his opposition to the Stamp Act, his support of the regulator expeditions but his distaste for further punishment of them, his role in the provincial congress but his January 9 letter), Moore evidenced the ambivalence of an ambitious man devoted to political order caught up in a revolutionary situation.

Local tradition holds that Maurice and his brother James died on the same day (January 15, 1777) in the same house, but there is some doubt about that claim. In any case, Maurice died sometime between January and April, 1777. His son, Alfred, became a justice of the United States Supreme Court in 1799.[42]

Despite their diverging arguments on parliamentary taxation, there are some striking similarities between Martin Howard and Maurice Moore. Both men were trained as lawyers, practiced for a time, and served as judges. Their writings, in the pamphlets and elsewhere, demonstrate a broad reading in the classics and history. That their educational backgrounds were similar is evident from their literary allusions, and each was schooled in New England. Both men were ambitious and sought high office as well as the approval of influential friends. Above all, Howard and Moore shared a fundamental conservatism. They loved order and dreaded any assault upon it. As justices at the trials of the regulators, they displayed similar views on the uprising as a threat to stability but later joined voices in calling for an end to further prosecution of the rebels. Each man approached the issue of parliamentary taxation from his basic conservatism. Howard viewed the American reaction as a danger to the established order of the British Empire; Moore saw such taxation as a menace to the venerable rights of English subjects. In each case, the two pamphleteers expressed a dread of change.

For all of their similarities, Howard and Moore had major differences, which, more than their similarities, determined why they viewed the question of parliamentary taxation so diversely. In his pamphlet Howard tended to argue philosophically while Moore concentrated on practical matters. Howard sought to justify representation as it had existed traditionally; Moore wanted to find solutions to the inadequate representation of colonial views in Parliament.

When one looks at the lives and careers of the two men, Howard seems consistent; Moore, contradictory. The former was a man of solid conservative principles from which he never deviated, even when faced by a violent mob in Newport or caught in the Revolution in North Carolina. All of his life

Howard admired the common law tradition of England. The crown was the embodiment of that tradition, and he would be loyal to it despite the personal cost. Moore, on the other hand, was faced with some difficult circumstances not confronting Howard. Unlike Howard, who was an outsider in North Carolina, Moore came from one of the leading families in the colony. His father had put down deep roots in the Lower Cape Fear region, and they anchored Moore solidly. His children and his brother were ardent patriots, but Maurice Moore's fundamental love of order led him to doubt their wisdom. As his letter to Josiah Martin dated January 9, 1776, shows, he dreaded the disruption that a civil war would bring. But faced with his family members' support of the Revolution, it was nearly impossible for him to desert them. In the face of such terrible choices, Moore's death in early 1777 was a merciful one.

When Howard and Moore wrote their pamphlets in 1765, they had no way of knowing what upheaval would occur in a mere decade. Once the Revolution began, Howard's consistency clarified his course of action; Moore's vacillation clouded his. While no historian can ever hope to know completely a figure from the past, this much is certain about Martin Howard and Maurice Moore: both men suffered profoundly for their choices — as did most Americans in 1776 whether loyalists or patriots.

---

[1] For the most authoritative collection of Revolutionary pamphlet literature as well as the best discussion of its impact, see Bernard Bailyn (ed.), *Pamphlets of the American Revolution, 1750-1776* (Cambridge: The Belknap Press of Harvard University Press, volume I, 1965), hereinafter cited as Bailyn, *Pamphlets of the American Revolution*; Bernard Bailyn, *The Ideological Origins of the American Revolution* (Cambridge: The Belknap Press of Harvard University Press, 1967), 1-4.

[2] Edmund S. and Helen M. Morgan, *The Stamp Act Crisis: Prologue to Revolution* (Chapel Hill: University of North Carolina Press, 1953), 53-70, 261-281, hereinafter cited as Morgans, *Stamp Act Crisis*.

[3] Morgans, *Stamp Act Crisis*, 294-295.

[4] John Russell Bartlett (ed.), *Records of the Colony of Rhode Island and Providence Plantations* (Providence: State Printer, 10 volumes, 1856-1865), IV, 375, hereinafter cited as Bartlett, *Rhode Island Records*; John W. Moore, *History of North Carolina* (Raleigh: A. Williams and Company, 2 volumes, 1880), I, 99.

[5] Henry Howard Edes, *Martin Howard Chief-Justice of North Carolina and His Portrait by Copley* (Cambridge: John Wilson and Son, 1903), 5, hereinafter cited as Edes, *Martin Howard*; Samuel A. Ashe and others

(eds.), *Biographical History of North Carolina: From Colonial Times to the Present* (Greensboro: Charles L. Van Noppen, 8 volumes, 1905-1917), III, 211, hereinafter cited as Ashe, *Biographical History*.

[6] Edes, *Martin Howard*, 5; William L. Saunders (ed.), *The Colonial Records of North Carolina* (Raleigh: State of North Carolina, 10 volumes, 1886-1890), IX, 6, hereinafter cited as Saunders, *Colonial Records*.

[7] Edes, *Martin Howard*, 5; Bartlett, *Rhode Island Records*, V, 386, 505; VI, 257, 336.

[8] Morgans, *Stamp Act Crisis*, 48-52; Bailyn, *Pamphlets of the American Revolution*, I, 529.

[9] Edmund S. Morgan (ed.), *Prologue to Revolution: Sources and Documents on the Stamp Act Crisis, 1764-1766* (Chapel Hill: University of North Carolina Press, 1959), 109-113, hereinafter cited as Morgan, *Prologue to Revolution*.

[10] Morgans, *Stamp Act Crisis*, 146.

[11] Morgan, *Prologue to Revolution*, 109-113.

[12] Bartlett, *Rhode Island Records*, VII, 216-217.

[13] Walter Clark (ed.), *The State Records of North Carolina* (Winston and Goldsboro: State of North Carolina, 16 volumes, numbered XI-XXVI, 1895-1907), XI, 209, hereinafter cited as Clark, *State Records*.

[14] Saunders, *Colonial Records*, VII, 427-428; Edes, *Martin Howard*, 8-9.

[15] Ashe, *Biographical History*, III, 213.

[16] Saunders, *Colonial Records*, VIII, 534; Ashe, *Biographical History*, III, 213.

[17] Saunders, *Colonial Records*, VIII, 169, 258.

[18] Howard to Charles Mellish, September 12, 1777, and memorial to Loyalist Claims Commission, February 20, 1783, in Loyalist Claims, British Audit Office Papers, Division of Archives and History, Raleigh.

[19] Lorenzo Sabine, *Biographical Sketches of Loyalists of the American Revolution with an Historical Essay* (Boston: Little, Brown and Company, 2 volumes, 1864), I, 547.

[20] Griffith J. McRee, *Life and Correspondence of James Iredell* (New York: D. Appleton-Century and Company, 2 volumes, 1857-1858), I, 364, hereinafter cited as McRee, *James Iredell*.

[21] Bailyn, *Pamphlets of the American Revolution*, I, 530; Edes, *Martin Howard*, 12.

[22] Allen Johnson, Dumas Malone, and others (eds.), *Dictionary of American Biography* (New York: Charles Scribner's Sons, 20 volumes, 1928), XIII, 133-134, hereinafter cited as Johnson and Malone, *Dictionary of American Biography*.

[23] Saunders, *Colonial Records*, V, 947-948; VI, 968.

[24] Saunders, *Colonial Records*, VI, 243, 365.

[25] Saunders, *Colonial Records*, VI, 1007.

[26] Lawrence Lee, "Days of Defiance: Resistance to the Stamp Act in the Lower Cape Fear," *North Carolina Historical Review*, XLIII (April, 1966), 192-196, hereinafter cited as Lee, "Days of Defiance."

[27] Lee, "Days of Defiance," 197-202.

[28] Saunders, *Colonial Records*, VII, 199-200.

[29] Marshall DeLancey Haywood, *Governor William Tryon and His Administration in the Province of North Carolina, 1765-1771* (Raleigh: E. M. Uzzell, 1903), 99-100, hereinafter cited as Haywood, *Governor Tryon*.

[30] Saunders, *Colonial Records*, VII, 829, 838-846.

[31] Saunders, *Colonial Records*, VIII, 178-179.

[32] Saunders, *Colonial Records*, VIII, 268-269, 494; Haywood, *Governor Tryon*, 107, 111. The Hunter-Moore letter is printed in William S. Powell

and others (eds.), *The Regulators in North Carolina: A Documentary History, 1759-1776* (Raleigh: Division of Archives and History, 1971), 277-280.

[33] Saunders, *Colonial Records*, VIII, 519-520, 534, 539, 694.

[34] Saunders, *Colonial Records*, VIII, 712; IX, 333-337.

[35] F. X. Martin, *The History of North Carolina from the Earliest Period* (New Orleans: A. T. Penniman and Company, 2 volumes, 1829), I, lvii. The Atticus letter is printed in Saunders, *Colonial Records*, VIII, 718-727.

[36] McRee, *James Iredell*, I, 201.

[37] Saunders, *Colonial Records*, X, 167, 173-175, 913.

[38] Ashe, *Biographical History*, II, 302-303.

[39] Saunders, *Colonial Records*, X, 395-396, 398-399.

[40] Clark, *State Records*, XI, 722.

[41] Saunders, *Colonial Records*, X, 431-432.

[42] Johnson and Malone, *Dictionary of American Biography*, XIII, 134; Ashe, *Biographical History*, II, 302-303; Lawrence Lee, *The Lower Cape Fear in Colonial Days* (Chapel Hill: University of North Carolina Press, 1965), 273.

Martin Howard
Photo: Archives and History

M artin Howard's A Letter from a Gentleman at Halifax to His Friend in Rhode Island *was written in February, 1765, to counter the arguments against parliamentary taxation made three months earlier in* The Rights of the Colonies Examined *by Rhode Island governor Stephen Hopkins. Howard probably authored the essay in Newport and used Halifax, Nova Scotia, in the title to refer to the establishment of the vice-admiralty court there in October, 1764 — a reference calculated to anger Rhode Island merchants. Although Howard's name did not appear on the title page, both his friends and enemies knew of his authorship soon after the pamphlet was printed.*

The work opens with a jab at Hopkins's prose style but shifts quickly into a refutation of the governor's argument that Parliament has no jurisdiction over the colonies. Howard distinguishes between the two kinds of rights which the provinces enjoy, personal and political. Personal rights of life, liberty, and estate (or property) belong to all British subjects by virtue of the common law — that vast unwritten body of precedent and tradition which has existed since before the Norman Conquest. Political rights in the colonies are set forth and limited in their original charters granted by the king. Howard argues that all American provinces are essentially corporations created by the crown, and they cannot enjoy any political rights not defined in their charters. While no colonist would wish to reject the common law, some Americans are embracing its provisions for personal rights without accepting one of its basic premises: that provinces are bound by acts of Parliament. To deny the jurisdiction of Parliament is to reject the common law.

Howard then argues in favor of the principle of virtual representation, the idea that every member of Parliament represents the whole of the British Empire not just the small constituency which elected him. Even if the colonies could elect a small number of members as does Scotland, how much influence would these men have in the whole of Parliament? Any change in the ancient system of government must be viewed as potentially dangerous. Howard says: "The goodly building of the British *constitution will be best secured and perpetuated by adhering to its original principles." The freedom of British subjects, whether English or American, depends not on having a representative from their local constituency but on the sense and virtue of Parliament as a whole. Once the jurisdiction of that body is admitted then its right to levy taxes is undeniable.*

Howard goes on to challenge Hopkins's allusions to ancient Greek and Roman tyrannies as having no application to the present situation in America. After all, the colonies of Greece and Rome had no charters defining their rights and delineating the duties of the mother country.

Near the end of the essay, Howard defends the establishment of a juryless admiralty court at Halifax to try American customs violators. Such a provision negates the corrupting influence which smugglers can have over local courts, and it benefits honest traders. Caustically, he points out that Hopkins governs a colony with countless smugglers. Howard also speaks of the governor's hypocrisy in espousing a self-righteous concern over the rights of the colonies when he presides over the most factious province in America.

Howard saves his most telling criticism of Hopkins for last. The current struggle between Britain and the colonies involves two problems: the jurisdiction of Parliament and the exercise of that jurisdiction. Hopkins ignores the distinction and deals only with the latter problem. Howard claims to prove the question of jurisdiction and, doing that, to settle the matter for all practical purposes.

The following rendition of Howard's pamphlet is literal; any misspellings or unusual punctuation in the original are repeated here. Page numbers as printed in the original are presented here in angle brackets. The present transcription is from a copy of the pamphlet belonging to the Louis R. Wilson Library of the University of North Carolina at Chapel Hill. A thoroughly annotated printing of this pamphlet appears in Bailyn's Pamphlets *of the American Revolution, I, 532-544. Footnotes added here either cover items which Bailyn did not annotate or which supplement his entries.*

A

LETTER

from a

Gentleman at *Halifax,*

to his

FRIEND in *Rhode-Island,*

containing

REMARKS upon a PAMPHLET,

entitled,

the rights of colonies

examined.

NEWPORT:
Printed and sold by S. HALL. m.dcc.lxv.

A
LETTER
FROM A
GENTLEMAN at *Halifax,*
TO HIS
FRIEND in *Rhode-Island,*
CONTAINING
REMARKS UPON A PAMPHLET,
ENTITLED,
THE RIGHTS OF COLONIES
EXAMINED.

NEWPORT:
PRINTED AND SOLD BY S. HALL.   M.DCC.LXV.

Original Title Page

A

LETTER, ETC.

HALIFAX, Nova-Scotia, January 20, 1765.

My Dear SIR,

I THANK you very kindly for the pamphlets and news-papers, you was so obliging as to send me. I will, according to your request, give you a few miscellaneous strictures on that pamplet wrote by Mr. H--p---s,[1] your governor, en-titled, "The rights of colonies examined."

His honour reminds me of the Roman poet. *"Est genus hominum, qui esse primos se omnium rerum volunt, / Nec sunt.---"/* He seems to give a solemnity to his performance, as if the subject had not been sufficiently handled by <4> any other before him, but I am of opinion he falls very short of Mr. -----, who, though unhappily misled by popular ideas, and at the head of the *tribunitian veto,* yet appears to be a man of knowledge and parts: Whereas *the rights of colonies examined,* is a laboured, ostentatious piece, discovers its author to be totally unacquainted with stile or diction, and eagerly fond to pass upon the world for a man of letters.

I cannot forgive the honourable author in adopting for his motto the three lines from *Thompson,*[2] so little applicable are they to the present times. I might challenge all the sons of discontent and faction, in the *British* dominions, to shew the least similitude between the years one thousand six hundred and forty-one, and one thousand seven hundred and sixty-four. How cruel and invidious is it to insinuate the most distant like-ness between the two periods? How much like sedition does it seem, to associate the present transactions of the nation with those of one thousand six hundred and forty-one, which soon after kindled into a civil war, and in the end overturned the *English* constitution?

The honourable author might perhaps flatter himself, that, in future editions of *Thompson's* liberty, commentators may insert *variae lectiones* of the text, and the three lines run thus: "Mid the low murmurs of submissive fear, / And mingled rage, my *H--p---s* rais'd his voice, / And to the laws appeal'd." / Or

19

perhaps some future bard may sing the present times, and HE be made the hero of the song. The aptness is easy and striking, and the idea too pleasing <5> to be resisted. *Narcissus*, in contemplating his own image, was turned into a daffodil. Who can think of this, and feel no pity for the pride and weakness of *man that is born of a woman.* "So have I seen, on some bright summer's day, / A calf of genius, debonnair and gay, / Dance on the brink, as if inspired by fame, / Fond of the pretty fellow in the stream." / LOVE OF FAME, THE UNIVERSAL PASSION.

I would fain hope that his honour's motto is not a true portrait of the general temper and conduct of the *Americans*; I would rather think *"the low murmurs of submissive fear, and mingled rage,"* delineate only a few disappointed traders. It were to be wished that some friend of the colonies would endeavour to remove any unfavourable impressions this, and other pamphlets of the like kind, may have occasioned at home; lest those in power form the general character of the colonies from such notices as these convey, and from thence be inclined to increase their dependance, rather than to emancipate them from the present supposed impositions. Depend upon it, my Friend, a people like the *English*, arrived to the highest pitch of glory and power, the envy and admiration of surrounding slaves, who hold the balance of *Europe* in their hands, and rival in arts and arms every period of ancient or modern story; a nation who, for the defence and safety of *America* only, staked their all in the late war; this people, I say, justly conscious of their dignity, will not patiently be dictated to by those whom they have ever considered as dependant upon them. Happy will it be for the colonies, yea happy for the honourable author, <6> if his pamphlet should meet with nothing more than contempt and neglect; for should it catch the attention of men in power, measures may be taken to stifle in the birth *"the low murmurs of submissive fear,"* and crush in embryo *"the mingled rage,"* which now so prettily adorns the head of his honour's pamphlet.

However disguised, polished or softened the expression of this pamphlet may seem, yet every one must see, that its professed design is sufficiently prominent throughout, namely, to prove, *that the colonies have rights independant of, and not controulable by, the authority of parliament.* It is upon this dangerous and indiscreet position I shall communicate to you my real sentiments.

To suppose a design of enslaving the colonies by parliament, is too presumptuous; to propagate it in print, is perhaps dangerous. Perplexed between a desire of speaking all he thinks, and the fear of saying too much, the honourable author is obliged to entrench himself in obscurity and inconsistency in several parts of his performance: I shall bring one instance.

In page eleven, he says, "It is the indispensible duty of every good and loyal subject chearfully to obey, and patiently submit to, all the laws, orders, etc. that may be passed by parliament."

I do not much admire either the spirit or composition of this sentence. Is it the duty *only* of good and loyal subjects to obey? Are the wicked and disloyal subjects absolved from this obligation? else why is this passage so marvellously penned: *Philolevtherus Lipsiensis* would directly pronounce this a figure in rhetorick, called nonsense. ---Believe me, my friend, I did not quote this passage to shew my skill <7> in criticism, but to point out a contradiction between it, and another passage in page twenty, which runs thus: "It must be absurd to suppose, that the common people of *Great-Britain* have a sovereign and absolute authority over their fellow subjects of *America, or even any sort of power whatsoever over them*; but it will be still more absurd to suppose, they can give a power to their representatives, which they have not themselves," etc. Here it is observable, that the first cited passage expresses a full submission to the authority of parliament; the last is as explicit a denial of that authority. The sum of his honour's argument is this: The people of *Great-Britain* have not any sort of power over the *Americans*; the house of commons have no greater authority than the people of *Great-Britain,* who are their constituents; *ergo* the house of commons *have not any sort of power over the* Americans. This is indeed a curious invented syllogism, the sole merit of which is due to the first magistrate of an *English* colony.

I have endeavoured to investigate the true natural relation, if I may so speak, between colonies and their mother state, abstracted from compact or positive institution, but here I can find nothing satisfactory; till this relation is clearly defined upon a rational and natural principle, our reasoning upon the

21

measure of the colonies obedience will be desultory and inconclusive. Every connection in life has its reciprocal duties; we know the relation between a parent and child, husband and wife, master and servant, and from thence are able to deduce their respective obligations; but we have no notices of any such precise natural relation between a mother state and its colonies, and therefore cannot reason with so much <8> certainty upon the power of the one, or the duty of the others. The ancients have transmitted to us nothing that is applicable to the state of modern colonies, because the relation between these is formed by political compact; and the condition of each variant in their original, and from each other. The honourable author has not freed this subject from any of its embarrassments: Vague and diffuse talk of rights and privileges, and ringing the changes upon the words liberty and slavery, only serve to convince us, that words may affect without raising images, or affording any repose to a mind philosophically inquisitive. For my own part, I will shun the walk of metaphysicks in my enquiry, and be content to consider the colonies rights upon the footing of their charters, which are the only plain avenues, that lead to the truth of this matter.

The several *New-England* charters ascertain, define and limit the respective rights and privileges of each colony, and I cannot conceive how it has come to pass that the colonies now claim any other or greater rights than are therein expresly granted to them. I fancy when we speak, or think of the rights of freeborn *Englishmen,* we confound those rights which are personal, with those which are political: There is a distinction between these, which ought always to be kept in view.

Our personal rights, comprehending those of life, liberty and estate, are secured to us by the common law, which is every subject's birthright, whether born in *Great-Britain,* on the ocean, or in the colonies; and it is in this sense we are said to enjoy all the rights and privileges of *Englishmen.* The political rights of the colonies, or the powers of government communicated <9> to them, are more limited, and their nature, quality and extent depend altogether upon the patent or charter which first created and instituted them. As individuals, the colonists participate of every blessing the *English* constitution can give them: As corporations created by the crown, they are confined within the primitive views of their institution. Whether therefore their indulgence is scanty or liberal, can be no cause of complaint; for when they accepted of their charters, they tacitly submitted to the terms and conditions of them.

The colonies have no rights independant of their charters, they can claim no greater than those give them, by those the parliamentary jurisdiction over them is not taken away, neither could any grant of the king abridge that jurisdiction, because it is founded upon common law, as I shall presently shew, and was prior to any charter or grant to the colonies: Every *Englishman*, therefore, is subject to this jurisdiction, and it follows him wherever he goes. It is of the essence of government, that there should be a supreme head, and it would be a solecism in politicks to talk of members independant of it.

With regard to the jurisdiction of parliament, I shall endeavour to shew, that it is attached to every *English* subject, wherever he be: And I am led to do this from a clause in page nine of his honour's pamphlet, where he says, "That the colonies do not hold their rights, as a privilege granted them, nor enjoy them as a grace and favour bestowed; but possess them, as an inherent, indefeasible right." This postulatum cannot be true with regard to political rights, for I have already shewn, that these are derived from your charters, and are held by force of <10> the king's grant; therefore these inherent, indefeasible rights, as his honour calls them, must be personal ones, according to the distinction already made. Permit me to say, that inherent and indefeasible as these rights may be, the jurisdiction of parliament, over every *English* subject, is equally as inherent and indefeasible: That both have grown out of the same stock, and that if we avail ourselves of the one, we must submit to, and acknowlege the other.

It might here be properly enough asked, Are these personal rights self-existent? Have they no original source? I answer, They are derived from the constitution of *England*, which is the common law; and from the same fountain is also derived the jurisdiction of parliament over us.

But to bring this argument down to the most vulgar apprehension: The common law has established it as a rule or maxim, that the plantations are bound by *British* acts of parliament, if particularly named: And surely no *Englishman*, in his senses, will deny the force of a common law maxim. One cannot but smile at the inconsistency of these inherent, indefeasible men: If one of them has a suit at law, in any part of *New-England*, upon a question of land property, or merchandize, he appeals to the common law, to support his claim, or defeat his adversary; and yet is so profoundly stupid as to say, that an act of parliament does not bind him; when, perhaps, the same page in a law book, which points him out a remedy for a libel, or a slap in the face, would inform him that it does.-----In a word, The force of an act of parliament, over the colonies, is predicated upon the common law, the origin and basis of all those inherent rights and privileges which constitute the boast and felicity of a *Briton.*

<11> Can we claim the common law as an inheritance, and at the same time be at liberty to adopt one part of it, and reject the other? Indeed we cannot: The common law, pure and indivisible in its nature and essence, cleaves to us during our lives, and follows us from *Nova Zembla* to *Cape Horn*: And therefore, as the jurisdiction of parliament arises out of, and is supported by it, we may as well renounce our allegiance, or change our nature, as to be exempt from the jurisdiction of parliament: Hence, it is plain to me, that in denying this jurisdiction, we at the same time, take leave of the common law, and thereby, with equal termerity and folly, strip ourselves of every blessing we enjoy as *Englishmen*: A flagrant proof this, that shallow draughts in politicks and legislation confound and distract us, and that an extravagant zeal often defeats its own purposes.

I am aware that the foregoing reasoning will be opposed by the maxim, "That no *Englishman* can be taxed but by his own consent, or by representatives."

It is this dry maxim, taken in a literal sense, and ill understood, that, like the song of *Lillibullero*,[3] has made all the mischief in the colonies: And upon this, the partizans of the colonies rights chiefly rest their cause. I don't despair, however, of convincing you, that this maxim affords but little support to their argument, when rightly examined and explained.

It is the opinion of the house of commons, and may be considered as a law of parliament, that they are the representatives of every *British* subject, wheresoever he be. In this view of the matter then, the aforegoing maxim is fully vindicated in practice, and the whole benefit of it, in substance and effect, extended and applied to the *colonies.* Indeed the maxim <12> must be considered in this latitude, for in a literal sense or construction it ever was, and ever will be, impracticable. Let me ask, is the isle of *Man, Jersey,* or *Guernsey,* represented?

24

What is the value or amount of each man's representation in the kingdom of *Scotland*, which contains near two millions of people, and yet not more than three thousand have votes in the election of members of parliament? But to shew still further, that, in fact and reality, this right of representation is not of that consequence it is generally thought to be, let us take into the argument the moneyed interest of *Britain*, which, though immensely great, has no share in this representation; a worthless freeholder of forty shillings *per annum* can vote for a member of parliament, whereas a merchant, tho' worth one hundred thousand pounds sterling, if it consist only in personal effects, has no vote at all: But yet let no one suppose that the interest of the latter is not equally the object of parliamentary attention with the former.----Let me add one example more: Copyholders in *England* of one thousand pounds sterling *per annum*, whose estates in land are nominally, but not intrinsically, inferior to a freehold, cannot by law, vote for members of parliament; yet we never hear that these people *"murmur with submissive fear, and mingled rage:"* They don't set up their private humour against the constitution of their country, but submit with chearfulness to those forms of government which providence, in its goodness, has placed them under.

Suppose that this *Utopian* privilege of representation should take place, I question if it would answer any other purpose but to bring an expence upon the colonies, unless you can suppose that a few *American* <13> members could bias the deliberations of the whole *British* legislature. In short, this right of representation is but a phantom, and, if possessed in its full extent, would be of no real advantage to the colonies; they would, like *Ixion*, embrace a cloud in the shape of *Juno*.

In addition to this head, I could further urge the danger of innovations; every change in a constitution, in some degree, weakens its original frame; and hence it is that legislators and statesmen are cautious in admitting them: The goodly building of the *British* constitution will be best secured and perpetuated by adhering to its original principles. Parliaments are not of yesterday, they are as antient as our *Saxon* ancestors. Attendance in parliament was originally a duty arising from a tenure of lands, and grew out of the feudal system; so that the privilege of sitting in it, is territorial, and confined to *Britain* only. Why should the beauty and symmetry of this body be destroyed, and its purity defiled, by the unnatural mixture of representatives from every part of the *British* dominions. *Parthians, Medes, Elamites, and the dwellers of Mesopotamia, etc.* would not, in such a case, speak the same language. What a heterogeneous council would this form? what a monster in government would it be?---In truth, my friend, the matter lies here: The freedom and happiness of every *British* subject depends, not upon his share in elections, but upon the sense and virtue of the *British* parliament, and these depend reciprocally upon the sense and virtue of the whole nation. When virtue and honour are no more, the lovely frame of our constitution will be dissolved. *Britain* may one day be what *Athens* and *Rome* now are; but may heaven long protract the hour!

<14> The jurisdiction of parliament being established, it will follow, that this jurisdiction cannot be apportioned; it is transcendent and entire, and may levy internal taxes as well as regulate trade; there is no essential difference in the rights: A stamp duty is confessedly the most reasonable and equitable that can be devised, yet very far am I from desiring to see it established among us, but I fear the shaft is sped, and it is now too late to prevent the blow.

The examples cited by his honour, with regard to ancient colonies, may shew his reading and erudition, but are of no authority in the present question. I am not enough skilled in the *Grecian* history to correct the proofs drawn from thence, though they amount to very little. If the *Grecian* colonies, as his honour says, "took such forms of government as themselves chose," there is no kind of similitude between them and the *English* colonies, and therefore to name them is nothing to the purpose. The *English* colonies take their forms of government from the crown; hold their privileges upon condition, that they do not abuse them; and hold their lands by the tenure of common socage, which involves in it fealty and obedience to the king: Hence it is plain, his honour's argument is not strengthened by the example of the *Grecian* colonies; for what likeness is there between independant colonies, as those must be, which "took such forms of government as themselves chose," and colonies like ours, which are in a manner feudatory, and holden of a superior.

With regard to the *Roman* colonies, I must beg leave to say, that the honourable author, either ignorantly or wilfully, mistakes the facts: A little more enquiry, or a little more candour, would have convinced <15> him, that the *Roman coloniae* did not enjoy all the rights of *Roman* citizens; on the contrary, they only used the *Roman* laws and religion, and served in the legions, but had not the right of suffrage, or of bearing honours. In these respects, our English colonies exactly resemble them; we enjoy the *English* laws and religion, but have not the right of suffrage, or of bearing honours in *Great-Britain,* and indeed our situation renders it impossible.

If the practice of the ancients was of any authority in this case, I could name examples to justify the enslaving of colonies. The *Carthaginians* were a free people, yet they, to render the *Sardinians* and *Corsicans* more dependent, forbad their planting, sowing, or doing any thing of the like kind, under pain of death, so that they supplied them with necessaries from Africa: This was indeed very hard. But there is something extremely weak and inconclusive in recurring to the *Grecian* and *Roman* history for examples to illustrate any particular favourite opinion: If a deference to the ancients should direct the practice of the moderns, we might sell our children to pay our debts, and justify it by the practice of the *Athenians.* We might lend our wives to our friends, and justify it from the Example of *Cato,* among the *Romans.* In a word, my dear Sir, the belly of a sow, pickled, was a high dish in ancient *Rome*; and I imagine, as you advance in the refinements of luxury, this will become a capital part of a *Rhode-Island* feast, so fond you seem of ancient customs and laws.

Instead of wandring in the labyrinth of ancient colonies, I would advise his honour to read the debates in parliament in the year one thousand seven hundred and thirty-three, when Mr. *Partridge,*[4] your agent, <16> petitioned the commons against the then sugar-bill; he will there find more satisfaction upon the subject of colonies, than in *Thucydides's history of the Pelopennesian war.* It was declared in the course of that debate, that the colonists were a part of the people of *Great-Britain*; and, as such, fully represented in that house. The petition then presented by Mr. *Partridge,* was of a very different temper from those now sent home by the colonies; it was extremely modest, and only intimated that the sugar bill, if passed into a law, might be prejudicial to their charter; at the bare mention of this Sir *William Yonge*[5] took fire, and said, *"It looked like aiming at an independency, and disclaiming the jurisdiction of that house, as if* (says he) *this house had not a power to tax the colonies." Mr. Winnington,*[6] with equal warmth, added, *"I hope they have no charter which debars this house from taxing them, as well as any other subject of the nation."* Here you have the opinion of two of the most eminent members of that time; they spoke the sentiments of the whole house, and these sentiments still continue the same. And from hence you may perceive, how little prospect there is of the colonies gaining any point upon the footing of these new supposititious rights; broaching such opinions will excite the jealousy of the parliament, and you will be looked upon with an evil eye. The promoters of such doctrines are no friends to the colonies, whatever may be their pretensions. Can his honour be so vain as to imagine, that ten thousand such pamphlets as his, will influence the parliament, or that they will be persuaded, by the force of his elocution, to give up their supremacy, and right of taxing the colonies. What purpose then can be served by these pamphlets, but to embitter the minds of a simple, credulous, and hitherto loyal people, <17> and to alienate their affections from *Great-Britain,* their best friend, their protector, and *alma mater.* A different behaviour would be much more prudent and politick. If we have any thing to ask, we should remember that diffidence and modesty will always obtain more from generous minds, than frowardness and impertinence.

The act of the thirteenth of his late majesty, entitled, *An act for naturalizing of foreign protestants,* had better have been omitted by his honour; for if that act is to be the measure of the colonists rights, they will be more circumscribed than he would willingly chuse. In that act, there is a proviso, that no person, who shall become a natural born subject by virtue of that act, should be of the privy council, or a member of either house of parliament, or capable of enjoying, in *Great-Britain* or *Ireland,* any place of trust, civil or military, etc. This statute confirms the distinction I have set up between personal and political rights. After naturalization, foreign protestants are here admitted subjects, to all intents and purposes; that is, to the full enjoyment of those rights which are connected with the person, liberty or estate of *Englishmen;* but by the proviso, they are excluded from bearing offices or honours.

Enlarging the power of the court of admiralty, is much complain'd of by the honourable author. I shall open my mind to you freely on this head.

It is notorious, that smuggling, which an eminent writer calls a crime against the law of nature, had well nigh become established in some of the colonies. Acts of parliament had been uniformly dispensed with by those whose duty it was to execute them; corruption, raised upon the ruins of duty and virtue, had almost grown into a system; courts of admiralty confined <18> within small territorial jurisdictions, became subject to mercantile influence; and the king's revenue shamefully sacrificed to the venality and perfidiousness of courts and officers. ---If, my friend, customs are due to the crown, if illicit commerce is to be put an end to, as ruinous to the welfare of the nation:---If, by reason of the interested views of traders, and the connivance of courts and custom-house officers, these ends could not be compassed or obtained in the common and ordinary way; tell me, what could the government do, but to apply a remedy desperate as the disease: There is, I own, a severity in the method of prosecution, in the new established court of admiralty, under Doctor *SPRY*,[7] here; but it is a severity we have brought upon ourselves. When every mild expedient, to stop the atrocious and infamous practice of smuggling, has been try'd in vain, the government is justifiable in making laws against it, even like those of *Draco*, which were written in blood. The new instituted court of admiralty, and the power given to the seizer, are doubtless intended to make us more circumspect in our trade, and to confine the merchant, from motives of fear and dread, within the limits of a fair commerce. "The *English* constrain the merchant, but it is in favour of commerce," says the admired *Secondat*. This is the spirit of the new regulations, both with regard to the employing of cutters, and the enlarged power of the admiralty; and both measures are justifiable upon the same principles, as is the late act for preventing murder, which executes and dissects the murderer at surgeons-hall in twenty-four hours after conviction.

But notwithstanding the severity of this act, let me add, that no harm can accrue to the honest and fair <19> trader, so long as the crown fills the admiralty department with an upright judge; such a one is Doctor *SPRY*, an able civilian, and whose appointments place him above any kind of influence; yet the honourable author of the pamphlet before me, has told us to this effect; That it is very well known this judge *can be prevailed on, very easily,* to certify, upon the acquittal of a seizure, that there was a probable cause for making it.----So shamefully intemperate is his honour's zeal and opposition to every measure adopted by the government at home, that he spares not even private characters, however worthy and respectable. I fear he knows not the high value of a good name, and how dear it is to men of sentiment and honour.

"He who filches from me my good name,
Robs me of that, which not enriches him,
But makes me poor indeed."

SHAKESPEAR.

To suspect the integrity of others, is not the effusion of a virtuous mind. Those who have been long used to traffick with judges and juries, are, from the depravity of their own hearts, easily led to believe others even as themselves.

This libel upon Doctor *SPRY*, contained in a pamphlet *published by authority*, may spread over the British dominions, and, however false and scandalous it be, yet may leave a shade upon his character which can never be effaced. With what grace, let me ask you, do such reflections as these come from the governor of a colony, where, all the world agree, the law has scarcely yet dawned, and where all your legal rights are decided by the strength of that faction which happens to be uppermost.

<20> I am not enough skilled in trade to know whether the act, so much complained of, will do most good or most harm; and I wish others were as diffident of their knowledge in this particular. To comprehend the general trade of the *British* nation, much exceeds the capacity of any one man in *America*, how great soever he be. Trade is a vast, complicated system, and requires such a depth of genius, and extent of knowledge, to understand it, that little minds, attached to their own sordid interest, and long used to the greatest licentiousness in trade, are, and must be, very incompetent judges of it. Sir *Andrew Freeport* is no inhabitant of *Rhode-Island* colony. For my own part, I am still willing to leave the management of trade with that people, who, according to the same admired author just quoted, "know better than any other people upon earth, how to value at the same time these three great advantages, religion, commerce, and liberty."

Here I would just observe, that, from the intelligence I have gained, the beloved article of melasses is now plentier and cheaper, in all the *New-England* colonies, than when it was avowedly smuggled; and so far is the linen manufacture of *Ireland* from being ruined, as his honour intimates, that never was a greater demand for flaxseed than during the last fall, notwithstanding the clause in the act relating to lumber. How senseless is it to imagine that the prohibiting a few dunnage staves to be carried to *Ireland,* will ruin the manufacturers of that kingdom.

Believe me, my Friend, it gives me great pain to see so much ingratitude in the colonies to the mother country, whose arms and money so lately rescued them from a *French* government. I have been told, that some have gone so far as to say, that they <21> would, as things are, prefer such a government to an *English* one.----Heaven knows I have but little malice in my heart, yet, for a moment, I ardently wish that these spurious, unworthy sons of *Britain* could feel the iron rod of a *Spanish* inquisitor, or a *French* farmer of the revenue; it would indeed be a punishment suited to their ingratitude. Here I cannot but call to mind the adder in one of the fables of *Pilpay,* which was preparing to sting the generous traveller who had just rescued him from the flames.

You'l easily perceive, that what I have said is upon the general design of his honour's pamphlet; if he had divided his argument with any precision, I would have followed him with somewhat more of method; The dispute between *Great-Britain* and the colonies consists of two parts; first, the jurisdiction of parliament,---and, secondly, the exercise of that jurisdiction. His honour hath blended these together, and no where marked the division between them: The first I have principally re-marked upon: As to the second, it can only turn upon the expediency or utility of those schemes which may, from time to time, be adopted by parliament, relative to the colonies. Under this head, I readily grant, they are at full liberty to remonstrate, petition, write pamphlets and newspapers, with-out number, to prevent any improper or unreasonable imposi-tion: Nay, I would have them do all this with that spirit of freedom which *Englishmen* always have, and I hope ever will, exert; but let us not use our liberty for a cloak of maliciousness. Indeed I am very sure the loyalty of the colonies has ever been irreproachable; but from the pride of some, and the ignorance of others, the cry against mother country has spread from colony to colony; <22> and it is to be feared, that prejudices and resentments are kindled among them which it will be difficult ever, thoroughly, to sooth or extinguish. It may become necessary for the supreme legislature of the nation to frame some code, and therein adjust the rights of the colonies, with precision and certainty, otherwise *Great-Britain* will always be teazed with new claims about liberty and privileges.

I have no ambition in appearing in print, yet if you think what is here thrown together is fit for the publick eye, you are at liberty to publish it: I the more chearfully acquiesce in this, because it is with real concern I have observed, that, notwithstanding the frequent abuse poured forth in pamphlets and news-papers against the mother country, not one filial pen in *America* hath, as yet, been drawn, to my knowledge, in her vindication.

I am, very affectionately,
Your most faithful and obedient servant,
****

F   I   N   I   S.

---

[1] Stephen Hopkins (1707-1785) became governor of Rhode Island in 1755 and served, with the exception of four years, until 1768. He was one of the signers of the Declaration of Independence. Johnson and Malone, *Dictionary of American Biography*, IX, 219-220.

[2] James Thomson (1700-1748), a Scotsman by birth and education, wrote most of his poetry in England. His five-part *Liberty* was published during 1735 and 1736. Leslie Stephen and Sidney Lee (eds.), *Dictionary of National Biography* (New York: Macmillan and Company, 73 volumes, 1885-1900), LVI, 246-254, hereinafter cited as Stephen and Lee, *Dictionary of National Biography*.

[3] "Lillibulero" was a poem by Thomas, Lord Wharton (1648-1715). Published in 1688 it was anti-tory and reflected support for William III in the Glorious Revolution. W. H. Auden (comp.), *The Oxford Book of Light Verse* (London: Clarendon Press, 1938), 191-192.

[4] Richard Partridge (1681-1759), a London merchant who acted as Rhode Island's agent to Parliament from 1715 through 1759. Michael G. Kammen, *A Rope of Sand: The Colonial Agents, British Politics and the American Revolution* (Ithaca: Cornell University Press, 1968), 319.

[5] Sir William Yonge (c. 1693-1755) was a member of the House of Commons from 1715 to 1755. Lewis Namier and John Brooke, *The House of Commons, 1754-1790* (New York: Oxford University Press, 3 volumes, 1964), III, 674.

[6] Thomas Winnington (1696-1746) was a member of the House of Commons from 1726 to 1741. Stephen and Lee, *Dictionary of National Biography*, LXII, 198-199.

[7] William Spry was first judge of the vice-admiralty court established for North America at Halifax, Nova Scotia, in October, 1764. Carl Ubbelohde, *The Vice-Admiralty Courts and the American Revolution* (Chapel Hill: University of North Carolina Press, 1960), 3-4.

Maurice Moore
Photo: Archives and History

M aurice Moore's The Justice and Policy of Taxing the American Colonies in England *was written in the summer of 1765 and printed in Wilmington. Unlike Martin Howard's work, it was not penned in direct reply to another pamphlet. Consequently, there is less personal comment and sarcasm in Moore's essay.*

He opens by tracing the origins of representative taxation in England prior to the Norman Conquest. The rights of a free British people have always prescribed that they not be required to render a portion of their private property to the community without their consent. Because American colonists settled the New World frontier at the crown's instigation, they are not a conquered people and enjoy the full birthright of British subjects. A cornerstone of that birthright is representative taxation.

Moore then goes on to challenge the doctrine of virtual representation. While it may have some validity in Great Britain where all countrymen reside in the same geographical unit, the colonies do not share in this physical proximity. In Britain those groups which cannot vote at least have a chance to know their parliamentary representative and to try to influence his views. Colonists enjoy no such opportunity. If virtual representation continues to exist, then Moore somewhat facetiously proposes that the provinces be separated into 558 districts (the number of seats in the House of Commons) and that each of these districts be assigned a present member of Parliament to whom they can make their views known. True representation does not depend on residence in a particular shire or borough but on certain kinds of tenure (ways of holding land). Various classes of tenure exist in America as surely as they do in England, and the colonists are just as entitled to representative government as are Englishmen. However, the present state of affairs is not equitable. Some satisfactory means of representing American views in the mother country must be worked out.

In order to encourage Englishmen to leave the security of their native land and venture into a virgin wilderness, the crown extended the full rights of its subjects to such settlers through charters. If Charles II had believed in virtual representation, he would never have specified that Carolinians be allowed to elect their own assembly in the charter of 1663. Moore contends that the idea of virtual representation is a new one designed to blunt American criticisms of parliamentary taxation. He argues that such taxation is not simply unjust but unwise, serving only to alienate the colonists' affection for the mother country. The Stamp Act, in particular, adds to the already heavy burden of British regulations on American commerce and might lead to a general collapse of trade. Unity between the colonies and the mother country would be good for both, but it can only come on terms of equality. He concludes by saying it is just that the provinces pay a portion of their own defense, but they must be allowed to consent to the way in which they pay.

The following rendition of Moore's pamphlet is literal. Page numbers of the original copy are here presented in angle brackets; Moore's references to specific sources are in square brackets. Transcription is from a copy of the pamphlet belonging to the Louis R. Wilson Library of the University of North Carolina at Chapel Hill. It has been printed previously in W. K. Boyd (ed.), Some Eighteenth Century Tracts Concerning North Carolina *(Raleigh: Edwards and Broughton Company, 1927), 159-174.*

THE

JUSTICE AND POLICY

of taxing

The AMERICAN COLONIES,

In GREAT BRITAIN, considered

Wherein is shewed,
That the Colonists are not a conquered People. That
they are constitutionally intituled to be taxed only by their
own Consent: -- And that the Imposing a Stamp Duty
on the Colonists Is as impolitic as it is inconsistant with
their Rights.

NON SIBI SED PATRIAE

By MAURICE MOORE, Esquire

WILMINGTON, (North-Carolina)

Printed by Andrew Steuart, and sold at his Office, near the

Exchange, M,DCC,LXV.

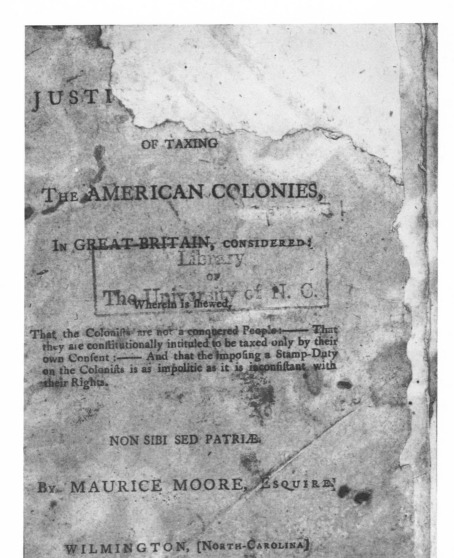

JUST[I]

OF TAXING

The AMERICAN COLONIES,

In GREAT-BRITAIN, CONSIDERED:

Wherein is shewed,

That the Colonists are not a conquered People: —— That they are constitutionally intituled to be taxed only by their own Consent :—— And that the imposing a Stamp-Duty on the Colonists is as impolitic as it is inconsistant with their Rights.

NON SIBI SED PATRIÆ.

By MAURICE MOORE, Esquire.

WILMINGTON, [North-Carolina]

Printed by Andrew Steuart, and sold at his Office, near the Exchange, M,DCC,LXV.

Original Title Page
Photo: Louis R. Wilson Library, University of North Carolina

The Justice and Policy of Taxing the American
Colonies in Great-Britain, considered.

WHETHER the Commons of England made up a part of the
Saxon Wittingham Mote, hath been a subject of great dispute;
and altho' this point has never been fully determined, yet it
seems to be agreed by the authority of two learned writers,
[Spellman and Maddox] that they were always called to attend
it, whenever the *exigencies* of the state made a tax *necessary*;
without doubt, to make known their circumstances, and to sug-
gest to that assembly some mode of taxation that was likely to
be the least burthensome to them. This just and laudable practice prevailed 'til the time of William the Conqueror, when
that prince erected a new court or parliament, of which the
commons were no part, and changed the Allodial tenure[1] of the
Saxons into the Feudal, and annexed certain rents or services
to all his grants, from which, together with fines and forfeitures,
the crown was abundantly supplied; it therefore seldom happened that any were taxed in this court; but when it did, they
were tallaged to one tenth part of their estate only, and none
but villeins were ever liable to be taxed at will.

This method of tallaging those who were subject to it, continued but for a few reigns after the conquest, and then a
regular parliament was established, which consisted of the
Superior and Inferior Barons, Citizens and Burgesses, who it is
said, [Ld. Coke] at first sat together: But when they had <4>
formed themselves into distinct houses, the representatives of
the people laid claim to their antient and equitable right of
taxing themselves and constituents, and have ever since, with
the greatest propriety and justice, enjoyed it.

From this slight view of the mode of imposing taxes for
public benefit, so long practised in Great-Britain, (in the course
of which there has been no other interruption, than that
occasioned by the conquest) it is clearly to be inferred, that
the right of prescribing the measure and manner of raising all
taxes is a constitutional one, which was enjoyed by the ancestors
of the Colonists; and the present inhabitants of Great-Britain,
as early as they have any knowledge of them from history, and
has been handed down to them under the influence of reason
and justice, through a course of several hundred years.

Nothing can be more consistent with the rights and liberties of a free people, than whenever the good of the community requires a part of the private property of Individuals, that they should be allowed to give it in such manner and portions as their situation and circumstances can best afford; indeed they cannot be free without it: for if any sublunary power in being, can deprive them of part of their estate without their consent, the same power may take away the whole; and if it appears to them to be a measure of justice, proscribe 'em into the bargain.

The inhabitants of the Colonies upon the Continent (other than those acquired in the late war) have always thought, and I believe ever will think, all the constitutional rights and liberties enjoyed <5> in Great-Britain, at the time they departed from it, their Birth-Right, and that they brought them over with them to America; among which, that of being taxed only by their own consent, is one of the most essential.

It is certainly very natural, that those who transport themselves from one country to another, should as well carry with them the Laws and Policy, as the Customs and Manners of the country from whence they came. But it hath been said from the authority of a very learned Judge, [Holt. Smith's case] that the Colonies are conquered countries; and that therefore the law is what the King pleases: but however learned and respectable the person might be who gave that opinion, I shall not hesitate to declare that I think the subject was not well considered and that it was founded on no Law whatever. Puffendorff,[2] in speaking of the different forms of government, takes occasion of mentioning two methods of treating the inhabitants of conquered countries; one is, when the victor removes 'em to his own country, or gives them the same privileges with his former subjects; the other is, when they are left to enjoy their antient seats, but entirely lose the sovereignty of the country. In this last case, he says, they are subject to the conqueror; but is the circumstance of any of the Colonies, other than those already excepted, similar to either of these cases? They surely are not. The antient inhabitants of the Colonies have neither been removed to Great-Britain, or left in possession of their lands; nor did they ever submit to, or acknowledge <6> themselves subject to any foreign power upon earth, but have long since abandoned the country, and retired into remote parts of America, where they are governed by their own laws and their own magistrates. It therefore cannot be said with the least

40

propriety, that the laws which these Savages alone, had they staid in the country, would have been liable to, as a vanquished people, are applicable to the present inhabitants of the Colonies, who themselves, are the conquerors. The earth, the air and trees, are by no means the object of any human laws whatsoever, otherwise than as they bear respect to the concernments of men. It must then be the conquered people, who are subject to the laws of the conqueror, and not the country.---The Colonists seem to stand on the same footing with those who leave their own country, and settle themselves in a new one which was not inhabited before: If they do, and I think it must appear so to any man who will give himself the trouble of considering this subject, then there is the opinion of the same learned Judge [Holt. Blankard's case] in favour of what I have advanced; which is that, the Colonists have brought over with them every constitutional right, liberty and privilege; and if being taxed only by their own consent is one of them, they cannot, with the least degree of justice, be taxed by the British parliament, in which they are not represented, no person in that assembly being authorized to signify their consent: Few persons there, are acquainted with their circumstance, and perhaps none know what mode of taxation would be least burthensome to them.

<7> It hath indeed pleased some of the honourable members of that august assembly to say, that the Colonies are virtually represented in parliament; but this is a doctrine which only tends to allow the Colonists a shadow of that *substance* which they must ever be slaves without. It cannot surely be consistent with British liberty, that any set of men should represent another, detached from them in situation and interest, without the privity and consent of the represented. The office of a repre-sentative is founded on choice, and is intended for the benefit of the constituents: A representative is to act in every respect as the persons who appointed him to that office would do, were they themselves present: And hath the members of the House of Commons, or any of them, been chose by the Colonists to represent them? Hath their conduct in respect to the Stamp Duty been consistent with the interests of the Colonists? or hath that conduct been such as the[y] the Colonists would have adopted, had they been present in parliament? No surely: So far from it, there are very few members of that assembly, who have ever been heard of in America. The Stamp Duty is inconsistent with their interests, and the mode of imposing it, destructive of their most essential rights and liberties. It is very fortunate for the present members of parliament, that for all that can be done in the Colonies, they have an estate for life in their office; for I believe I may venture to say, that no Colonist in his senses, would ever desire to be again represented by the same people.

To prove that the Colonists are within the <8> meaning of the doctrine of virtual representation, they have been compared to the inhabitants of several corporate towns in England, to the East-India company, the body of London merchants, to the proprietors of the public funds, to women and children, and in short, to all those who do not vote for the electing of members of parliament, who are all said to be virtually represented: On the justice and truth of this comparison intirely depends the decision of this question. It may therefore be necessary to observe, that by the antient English constitution, none were actually represented in parliament, other than Shires, the Cinque-Ports, Cities, and Antient Boroughs, and the elections for them were made by freeholders, and those who held by free burgage tenure; all villeins, copyholders, tenants and antient demesne, and tenants-of-lords, were excluded from electing or being elected: but at latest, in King John's time, a practice obtained of making free boroughs by charter, by which means they became intitled to send members to parliament, and it continued till the reign of King Charles the Second, when the House of Commons voted the elections made by virtue of that King's charters void, and so put a stop to the practice. From hence it is evident that the right that those derive from their particular species of property, peculiar franchises, and inhabitancy in particular places, is not an exclusive one, because it either depends on that which may, through the bounty of the crown, be extended, at least to its American subjects, or on a certain species of property that may be bought and sold, <9> and which the Colonists are capable of possessing in any part of the King's dominions. If the right of being actually represented in parliament, is constitutionally annexed to freehold estate, the American freeholders can with no more justice be deprived of it, than they may of their freeholds. And the power of dispossessing them of either, cannot, from the nature of the British constitution, (which is formed on the foundation of securing to every individual his right, liberty and property) be lodged with any other persons in being, than themselves: The acknowledging them to have a right of being taxed only by their own consent, is yielding them that from which they never can derive the least advantage, while ever that of actually choosing their own representatives, is withheld from them.

The notion of virtual representation, may, for all I know, be consistent enough, while it is confined to Great-Britain only; its inhabitants intimately reside together; the interest and circumstance of those who do not vote for representatives, are the same with those that do; and are equally well known to, and understood by such representatives. It cannot then be imagined that the virtually represented in Great Britain can ever be subject to any imposition, that will not be extended to, and equally affecting to the electors of members of parliament: And tho' certain corporate towns, the East-India company, the body of London merchants, proprietors of public funds, the monied interest, and women are respectively as such, actually represented in parliament; yet many of the members of them (women excepted) are intitled to vote for representatives; < 10 > and if they were not, the influence they, and particularly women (through whose means votes are often obtain'd) must necessarily have, from their intimate acquaintance and connection with the electors, is such as must render the choice in a great measure agreeable to them. But hath the Colonies any of these advantages? They certainly have not: They live above a thousand leagues from Great-Britain; their interest and circumstance are not similar to those of the British inhabitants; nor have they been well considered or understood by the British parliament. The Colonists have suffered many impositions, as may be seen by the several acts of trade which have been borne by them alone, and which no otherwise affected the electors of members of parliament, than as they were obliged to receive the profit arising from them. The Colonists cannot have the least influence either with the electors or elected, they are almost unknown to either of them, unless as mere vehicles of trade; in which light indeed they have been long known and considered.

If those who have been for bringing the Colonies within the meaning of virtual representation, by comparing them to certain corporate towns and persons in England, had been pleased to mention why those places and people are virtually represented in parliament, they must at the same time have proved that there is no similitude between them and the Colonies; for all these places lay, and body of men reside in, some county or other of Great-Britain; and tho' nine tenths of the inhabitants of any county should not be intitled to vote at an election, yet are they a part of that county, and as such, may be virtually <11> represented by those who have been elected to represent the whole county: But here the virtually represented know their representatives, and may, indiscriminately with the freeholders, at any time, instruct them what part to act in cases of importance: But I should be glad to be informed, in what county in England the Colonies are situated? If in no one at all; who are their particular virtual representatives? To say that they are represented by the whole body of the House of Commons, will be to leave them without that advantage of giving their representatives occasional instructions, which the virtually represented in England have; for it cannot be imagined, that the conduct of the House of Commons can ever be subject to the direction of the Colonists. The same reason then why certain persons in England (who have been excluded from voting at elections, merely for conveniency) may be virtually represented in parliament, doth not hold good in respect of the Colonies; I therefore conclude that they cannot be represented in the same manner: But if it should be still insisted upon, that they are, I would then humbly propose, that the Colonies be divided into five hundred and fifty-eight districts, and that each of them be numbered; that for the future, all writs of election in England, shall direct the voters to chuse a person to sit and vote in parliament as real representative of the county, city, or borough, for which such writ shall be issued; and as virtual representative of the five hundred and fifty-eighth part of the Colonies of such a number; and that each district be made acquainted with its particular virtual representative. <12> By this means the Colonists will know, to whom they are to direct their instructions; and will so far be upon a footing with the virtually represented in Great-Britain. That the notion of the Colonists being virtually represented in parliament, is of late date, is evident from the numberless acts of oppression and tyranny that have been practised upon them by officers of the crown commissioned in England, and sent over to America, which have been repeatedly made known, and complained of in England; and whenever it hath happened that they were conveyed

44

to the Royal Ear in Council, it hath constantly been thro' the channel of the Board of Trade: But in no one instance, that I know of, did ever the British parliament represent to the crown any grievances felt only in the Colonies, or make application to the Sovereign for a redress of them, and as a grand inquest for the whole kingdom, (had they thought themselves the representatives of the Colonies) they would never have negligently passed over a duty which was indispensibly incumbent upon them. And that the British parliament doth take cognizance of such subjects, when they happen ir Great-Britain, is undeniably true; and would it not be want of humanity, to suppose that they have always considered themselves as the representatives of the Colonies, and yet have ever neglected to render them an essential service, to which all those they represent, are indisputably intitled. To the inhabitants of the Colonies I have been speaking of, the crown has been graciously pleased to grant respectively the plans of exercising their constitutional rights, < 13 > I have now before me a Charter given by King Charles the Second to the province of Carolina,[3] and observe, one of the principal objects of this Charter, was to encourage the settlement of that colony, in which few resided at the time it was granted; nor was it then likely that many would leave their native country, wherein they enjoyed every right and liberty an excellent constitution could afford, and come over to the desarts of America, unless by some means or other, an enjoyment of those rights and liberties in Carolina, could be secured to them and their posterity: One of these was, to be taxed only by their own consent, signified in parliament by representatives actually chosen by themselves; and as the remote situation of Carolina from Great-Britain, rendered it imposible for those who should inhabit that province, to run over to England whenever a new parliament was to be summoned.--- King Charles thought proper to grant, that an assembly should be called and established by the proprietors, and that the freemen of Carolina, should consent, by themselves, or deputies in that assembly, to all laws whatsoever, that might respect the public state of the whole province or territory, or of any distinct or particular county. And had the crown considered the Colonists as being virtually represented in parliament, such a grant would have been extremely absurd; for no set of people can be represented at one time in two distinct and independent assemblies, which may counteract each other: This might be to make the represented grant and refuse in one instant the same thing, which is impossible, from the nature of the human <14> mind. That it is a matter intirely new in England, further appears, from the constant and repeated applications that have been made by the Crown in the course of the last war, to the assemblies in the Colonies, for supplies; which, if the British parliament could have given, might as easily have been asked for in England; and in all probability, would have been much more liberally granted; but the parliament had not then imagined themselves the representatives of the Colonists; if they had, would they not have interposed and asserted their right of taxing their constituents? more especially, as the poverty of the Colonists often obliged them to grant much less than the Crown required, and the burthen became proportionably heavier in Great-Britain, as it was lighter in America; would they not have acquainted the King that they were the Colony representatives, and that the Colonists might be much more copiously taxed in parliament, than it was likely they wou'd choose to be, if their consent was to be asked in their own provincial assemblies? Without doubt they would; but the truth is, the notion of their being virtually represented, had not then an existence, but [which had] been since introduced, to cover the shackles which have been prepared for the Colonists in their present state of inability, by those, who being wholly attentive to themselves, forget that the Colonists are their fellow-subjects; that they were born free, and are intitled to every British constitutional right and liberty, as well as themselves; or that to do them injustice, is as criminal, as to deal unjustly with those they really represent. To impose a Tax on the Colonies, in the British parliament, appears to me, to be a measure almost as impolitic, as it is inconsistent with the rights of the Colonists; <15> for as they are unalterably of opinion, that such an imposition is no less arbitrary than oppressive, it will by degrees alienate their affections from the Mother Country; the seeds of discontent will be sowed in the Colonies, and children will be taught to hate the name of those who have enslaved their country; the principles of disaffection will increase with their years, and the spirit of rebellion grow formidable with their numbers; and in the course of a century or two, it will cost Great-Britain more to keep them in their state of subjection, than all the profits arising from them, will pay: And if it did not, the story of Julius Caesar, is enough to shew that there is danger in a standing army abroad.

The Stamp Duty is itself a burthen too great for the circumstances of the Colonies to bear, considering the many restrictions that have been put upon their trade, which are at present rigorously enforced throughout America: It will occasion a discontinuance of industry, and must in the end, reduce them to a state of beggary; they will no longer be able to purchase the manufactures of the Mother Country, or furnish her with materials for making new ones. Great Britain then loses a trade, from which she hath derived her greatest opulence and dignity, and this too by insisting on a measure destructive of the peace and happiness of many thousands of as loyal subjects as any the King has. Can this be consistent with the wisdom and humanity of a British parliament? I think it cannot. The act imposing a Stamp Duty will surely be repealed, as soon its consequences are well considered. I am persuaded, the more closely united the Mother Country and the Colonies are, the happier it will be for both; but such an union will never take effect, but upon a foundation of equality: They must be upon such a footing, as that each may advance the other's interest, while he labours for his own. A very sensible and elegant writer [Cato's Letters] in speaking of Colonies, hath observed that, "It is not to be hoped, in the corrupt state of human nature, that any nation will be subject to another, any longer than it finds its own account in it, and cannot help itself. Every man's first thought will be for himself and his own interest; and he will not be long to seek for arguments to justify his being so, when he knows how to attain what he proposes. Men will think it hard to work, toil, and run hazards, for the advantage of others, any longer than they find their own interest in it; and especially for those <16> who use them ill: All nature points out that course. No creature sucks the teats of their dams, longer than they can draw milk from thence, or can provide themselves with better food; nor will any country continue their subjection to another, only because their great grand-mothers were acquainted. This is the course of human affairs; and all wise states will always have it before their eyes. They will well consider, therefore, how to preserve the advantages arising from Colonies, and avoid the evil. And I conceive that there can be but two ways in nature to hinder them from throwing off their dependence; one to keep it out of their power, and the other out of their will. The first must be by force, and the latter by using them well, and keeping them employed in such producions, and making such manufactures as will support themselves and families comfortably, and procure them wealth too; or at least, not prejudice their Mother Country,--Force can never be used effectually to answer the end, without destroying the Colonies themselves. Liberty and Encouragement are necessary to carry people thither; and violence will hinder both, etc." ---I do not pretend to be politician enough to point out the methods that will most effectually secure the dependency of the Colonies; but I am as much convinced that just and equitable ones may be discovered and pursued, as I am, that force and oppression will one day or other, produce a contrary effect. It would be no injustice that the Colonies should bear a proportionable part of the heavy expence that hath been incurred in the course of the late war; and I am persuaded, that no man of sense in the Colonies would oppse it; but they should be allowed to consent to it, according to their constitutional right, in their own provincial assemblies, where they are really represented: And in estimating such proportion of expence, their number, circumstance, and the restrictions on their trade, should be considered: But if the British parliament will insist on taxing the Colonists, as their virtual representatives, then are they stripped of that constitutional right on which their liberty and property depends, and reduced to the most abject state of slavery: A situation, in which, it is very unnatural to think, a Mother can take pleasure in viewing her children.

END.

[1] Free tenure, held without any obligation of vassalage or fealty. Henry C. Black, *Black's Law Dictionary* (St. Paul: West Publishing Company [Fourth Edition], 1951), 100.

[2] Samuel von Pufendorf (1632-1694), German jurist, historian and natural law philosopher. *Encyclopedia Britannica* (Chicago: Encyclopedia Britannica, Incorporated, 30 volumes, [Fifteenth Edition], 1974), VIII, 293.

[3] Moore refers to the charter issued to the Lords Proprietors on March 24, 1663. It is printed in Mattie Erma Parker (ed.), *North Carolina Charters and Constitutions, 1578-1698* (Raleigh: Carolina Charter Tercentenary Commission, 1963), 74-89.

About the Author

The author-editor of *Not a Conquered People*, William S. Price, Jr., is a native North Carolinian. Graduating from Duke University in 1963 with an A.B. in History, he served three years as an officer in the U. S. Navy, with Vietnam service. Price took his M.A. in U. S. History at the University of North Carolina at Chapel Hill in 1969 and his Ph.D. there in 1973. He is currently Head, Colonial Records Branch, Division of Archives and History, Raleigh. His publications include *North Carolina Higher-Court Records, 1702-1708.*